CT Martin's Superheros

A Collaboration by the amazing students that attend the
CT MARTIN Afterschool Program

3G Publishing, Inc.
Loganville, Ga 30052
www.3gpublishinginc.com
Phone: 1-888-442-9637

First published by 3G Publishing, Inc. August, 2024.

ISBN: 9781941247815

Printed in the United States of America

CT Martin's Superheros

A Collaboration by the amazing students that attend the
CT MARTIN Afterschool Program

AND THE FUN BEGINS!

Coach Mike was like a wizard guiding his young apprentices into a realm of endless imagination. The kids' eyes sparkled with anticipation as Coach Mike unveiled the thrilling adventures awaiting them in his after-school activities at CT Martin.

Spending time with Coach Mike was the best fun the kids would have all week. They ran relay races, played spelling games, won prizes, and learned to have an imagination to create comic books.

Coach Mike plunged the kids into a world of comic book magic, helping them dream up epic superheroes and dastardly villains, sparking wild adventures and daring rescues in their minds.

The kids were pumped up by Coach Mike's lively and out-of-the-box ideas, sparking their imagination to dive into the exciting world of creating their very own comic book masterpiece!

Together, they cooked up quirky characters, mapped out a thrilling plot, and sprinkled artistic magic on every page.

As the sun set on their epic nine-week journey at CT Martin, the kids beamed with pride as they handed over their masterpiece comic book to Coach Mike. His eyes widened in astonishment at their skill and commitment, vowing to treasure their creation in the rec center library for all to marvel at.

WOW

From that moment on, Coach Mike transformed into a superstar at the rec center, capturing Deandre's heart who hoped he'd stick around forever. The gang worshipped him for his boundless enthusiasm, passion for play, and rock-solid backing of their wildest dreams. With Coach Mike in the mix, their escapades had no expiration date in sight!

HEY!

AWESOME!

"People don't realize how a man's life can be changed by one book."
-Malcolm X

www.ingramcontent.com/pod-product-compliance
Lightning Source LLC
LaVergne TN
LVHW070839080426
835511LV00025B/3487

9 781941 247815